THE

RUGBY

LOVER'S
COMPANION

THE RUGBY LOVER'S COMPANION

Summersdale Publishers Ltd
46 West Street
Chichester
West Sussex
PO19 1RP
UK

www.summersdale.com

Printed and bound by CPI Group (UK) Ltd, Croydon, CR0 4YY

ISBN: 978-1-84953-173-3

THE
RUGBY
LOVER'S
COMPANION

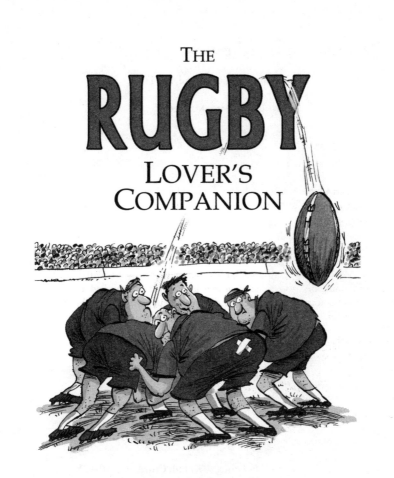

Steven Gauge

Illustrations by Ian Baker

summersdale

CONTENTS

INTRODUCTION

'This stone commemorates the exploit of William Webb Ellis who with a fine disregard for the rules of football as played in his time first took the ball in his arms and ran with it thus originating the distinctive feature of the rugby game. AD 1823'

Inscription on a plaque at Rugby School

When William Webb Ellis first picked up the ball on a playing field at Rugby School it is unlikely he would have quite imagined what he was starting. One floppy-haired public schoolboy's little act of rebellion launched a game that is played by nearly three million people in Great Britain and Ireland put together and by millions more in over ninety countries all around the world.

The Webb Ellis story may owe more to Rugby School's early spin doctors than the sports historians, but the school can certainly lay claim to an early set of rules for the sport that bears its name. (It might be nice if, one day, some of the referees I play under got round to reading them.) Thousands of British and Irish schools are now rugby-playing schools and nearly three thousand local rugby clubs put out one or more teams every week through the autumn and winter months of the year.

Young Webb Ellis cannot however be held entirely responsible for the monumental quantities of alcohol consumed in celebration of great rugby victories, or to drown the sorrows of defeated sides. A beer-soaked drinking culture has ensured that rugby players' and their supporters' livers have collectively taken their fair share of punishment in the best interests of the sport.

With the home nations of Scotland, England, Wales and Ireland all participating at the highest levels, rugby unites the British Isles like no other sport. In the southern hemisphere, the great rugby nations of Australia, New Zealand and South Africa have created sporting rivalries and friendships that reach right around the globe. Down to the smallest local club, with a role for players of all shapes and sizes, rugby brings people from all walks of life together for a great game, great drama and great camaraderie.

Football may claim to be the 'beautiful game' but rugby truly is a mighty sport.

FROM CHASING PIGS' BLADDERS TO WINNING WORLD CUPS

Rugby is a good occasion for keeping thirty bullies far from the centre of the city.

Oscar Wilde

ON THE PLAYING FIELDS OF RUGBY SCHOOL

The game we now know as rugby grew out of the traditional football games played throughout England in the Middle Ages. Huge mobs of unlimited numbers would compete to kick or drag an inflated pig's bladder from one end of a town or village to the other. This sort of chaotic, drunken marauding was exactly the sort of thing the people who decided to introduce the Modern Era wanted to stamp out. It fell to those fine institutions, the public schools of England, to refine, regulate and reform the games into a respectable pastime for gentlemen. As schools such as Winchester and Eton were founded around the turn of the fifteenth century, young aristocrats adapted the games for their school playing fields. Eton's version was known as the Wall Game, which sadly doesn't seem to have caught on elsewhere, presumably owing to the lack of suitable walls. However, those fine chaps at Rugby School came up with a version which was much easier to replicate. By 1845 three pupils had sat down and written the rules, although, even now, very few forwards have learnt how to read them. Clutching dog-eared copies of the 'Rugby School Rules', players grew up, moved away and formed clubs of their own around the world.

In 1871 the Rugby Football Union was formed. The rules became 'laws', drafted by three lawyers, who also happened to be former Rugby School pupils. More clubs were formed and crowds grew and grew.

In 1878, for example, a crowd of over 8,000 people watched Broughton beat Swinton at the Yew Street Ground in Salford, Greater Manchester, in the first recorded match played under floodlights. Rugby provided a lively source of entertainment for large working-class crowds when the alternatives in that year, towards the tail end of the Industrial Revolution, appeared to be joining the newly formed Salvation Army, falling off collapsing railway bridges or catching typhoid.

One possible reason why rugby caught on so fast could be down to the hugely popular novel *Tom Brown's Schooldays*, first published in 1857. Written by former Rugby School pupil Thomas Hughes and based largely on his own experience, the novel contains a vivid description of the game that so dominated the school.

RUGBY TIMELINE

1823 – William Webb Ellis first picks up the ball and runs with it

1843 – Guy's Hospital Rugby Club formed

1845 – First set of rules published by Rugby School

1871 – Rugby Football Union formed

1875 – Teams reduced to fifteen-a-side

1878 – Cardiff side invent the 'flying half back', which later becomes the 'fly half'

1883 – First sevens tournament in Melrose, Scotland

1884 – First New Zealand tour to New South Wales, Australia

1885 – Referee's whistle introduced

1886 – International Rugby Board formed (England refuse to join until 1890)

1888 – British and Irish Lions tour Australia and New Zealand

1893 – Payments to players to compensate for loss of earnings blocked by the RFU

1895 – Twenty-two Northern clubs break away to allow player payments, leading to the development of the alternative code of rugby league

1903 – New Zealand play their first international game against Australia

1905 – All Blacks tour British Isles

1907 – RFU committee member Billy Williams buys 10¼ acres of market garden in Twickenham, South West London

1910 – First international to be played at Twickenham (England v Wales)

1938 – First international to be broadcast live on TV (England v Scotland)

1939–45 – During World War Two, Twickenham was used as a civil defence depot and the car park was dug up for allotments

1968 – Replacement of injured players allowed – two per team

1969 – Anti-apartheid demonstrations as South Africa tour UK

1987 – First World Cup Tournament held in Australia and New Zealand

1995 – Rugby union becomes professional

2003 – England become the first Northern Hemisphere side to win the World Cup

2006 – Twickenham South Stand reopens, taking the ground's capacity to 82,000

In 1823, William Webb Ellis first picked up the ball in his arms and ran with it. And for the next 156 years forwards have been trying to work out why.

Sir Tasker Watkins (1979)

The ball rolls slowly in behind the School-house goal not three yards in front of a dozen of the biggest School players-up.

There stand the School-house praepostor, safest of goal-keepers, and Tom Brown by his side, who has learned his trade by this time. Now is your time, Tom. The blood of all the Browns is up and the two rush in together and throw themselves on the ball, under the very feet of the advancing column; the praepostor on his hands and knees arching his back, and Tom all along on his face. Over them topple the leaders of the rush, shooting over the back of the praepostor, but falling flat on Tom and knocking all the wind out of his small carcase. 'Our ball,' says the praepostor, rising with his prize; 'but get up there, there's a little fellow under you.' They are hauled and roll off him, and Tom is discovered a motionless body.

Old Brooke picks him up. 'Stand back, give him air,' he says; and then feeling his limbs, adds, 'No bones broken. How do you feel, young un?'

'Hah-hah,' gasps Tom as his wind comes back, 'pretty well, thank you – all right.'

'Who is he?' says Brooke. 'Oh, it's Brown, he's a new boy; I know him,' says East, coming up.

'Well, he is a plucky youngster, and will make a player,' says Brooke.

From *Tom Brown's Schooldays* by Thomas Hughes

THE FIRST INTERNATIONAL

England and Scotland staged the first international rugby
union fixture in Edinburgh in 1871. There had been
a soccer international the year before, which Scotland
had lost. The Scots' reaction was to declare rugby their
preferred game and to issue an invitation to England to
join them for a game in Edinburgh in March 1871.
With twenty players on each side the game consisted of
one long rolling maul. Under the rules of the time, points
could only be scored by kicking the ball between the posts.
Touching the ball down behind the opponents' goal line
entitled a team to 'try' for a goal.
Scotland pushed a scrum over the try line and fell on the
ball and as a result converted the only points of the game.
Referees did not feature in the early years of the games,
with most decisions being agreed between the captains.
Disputes were resolved by the umpire on the touchline, in
this case Dr H. H. Almond, a local headmaster. When in
doubt, he used the following rule of thumb:
'When an umpire is in doubt, I think he is justified in
deciding against the side which makes the most noise.
They are probably in the wrong.'
After the game, England officials proposed using
neutral referees, a practice which was introduced the
following year.

POSITIONS, PLEASE!

The Holy Writ of Gloucester
Rugby Club demands: first, that
the forwards shall win the ball;
second, that the forwards shall
keep the ball; and third, the backs
shall buy the beer.

Doug Ibbotson

A CYNIC'S GUIDE TO RUGBY POSITIONS

One of the many joys of rugby is that there is a place for almost everyone in a team. The positions around the pitch each require a specific physique and technique. As a result, particular personalities seem to attach themselves to the different shirt numbers.

PART 1: FORWARDS

1. LOOSE-HEAD PROP

This is the prop on the left-hand side of the front row – so called because his head is on the outside of the scrum as the two packs come together. Props are typically the stouter members of the team, often with little that could be reasonably described as a neck. Aside from front-row duties, they are normally allocated line-out lifting duties and forgiven for a lack of pace. Many can quite happily go through an entire season without touching the ball. If they do ever get the ball in hand they are very unlikely to know what to do with it.

2. HOOKER

The smallest forward, found in the middle of the front row, in the middle of the scrum. His job is to hook the ball back when it is put into the scrum, hence the name. He normally also throws the ball in from line-outs and as a result gets to touch the ball ever so slightly more often than props. A great job for hobbits.

3. TIGHT-HEAD PROP

Found on the right-hand side of the front row and, as the scrum is formed, his head is nestled in between the opposition loose head and hooker. His main reason for living is to make life difficult for the opposition hooker and in the meantime has to stop the scrum from collapsing. A lifter in the line-out and, as with the loose-head prop, he seems to harbour a secret ambition to kick a winning drop goal in the dying moments of a game – and perhaps, as a result, resorts to comfort eating to overcome his perpetual disappointment.

4 AND 5. SECOND ROW (OR 'LOCKS')

Home for the tallest, strongest and bravest, but not necessarily the brightest, players on the pitch. They may not have started out in life's slow stream but years of having their brain squashed between the front row's backsides may have taken its toll. If they have kept the weight down, they might also be lifted in the air in the line-out and be expected to catch the ball. Broken noses and cauliflower ears are common identifying features.

6 AND 7. FLANKERS

Historically known as wing forwards, these are the more agile of the forwards, normally found hanging loosely off the sides of the scrum, heads poking up like meerkats waiting for the opportunity to break away and attack the opposition backs. Expected to be strong, fearless tacklers and good ball carriers, the role offers a good home for anyone with anger management issues.

NUMBER 8

The only position with just a number rather than a name, positioned at the back of the scrum and typically home to the forward who can combine brain and brawn. Has the option to pick up the ball from the back of the scrum or feed it out to the backs. Needs to have a good tactical understanding of the game and the ability to carry the ball and crash through opposition defences. Best not to say anything rude about them whatsoever.

Playing in the second row doesn't require a lot of intelligence really. You have to be bloody crazy to play there for a start.

England second-row legend Bill Beaumont

Forwards are the gnarled and scarred creatures who have a propensity for running into and bleeding all over each other.

Peter Fitzsimmons

PART 2: BACKS

> Rugby backs can be identified because they generally have
> clean jerseys and identifiable partings in their hair... come the
> revolution, the backs will be the first to be lined up against the
> wall and shot for living parasitically off the work of others.
>
> Peter Fitzsimmons

9. SCRUM HALF

Little chap, who for some reason thinks he is a forward. Not unlike a Jack Russell with personality problems, nipping and yapping away behind any scrum, ruck or maul. Needs to be someone who can pass the ball quickly and accurately but has normally developed these skills out of necessity, to avoid being marmalised by marauding flankers.

10. FLY HALF

The poster boys of the side, close enough to the action to be able to show off their skills but far enough away to avoid too much collateral damage. Also known as the 'stand-off' because of their position standing a safe distance away from the forwards waiting for the ball to emerge. They marshal the backs to prepare for a series of complex moves, most of which never see the light of day as the forwards either keep the ball to themselves or lose it to the opposition. Kicking skills are essential for getting the side out of trouble and converting tries. Their kitbag will almost certainly contain the most hair products and body spray of any members of the team.

11 AND 14. WINGERS

The place for someone who can run fast but really would rather avoid any of that tackling malarkey. They don't need to be able to pass or kick, as it's very unlikely they will ever get the ball. If they do get the ball it will be at the end of a rare, successful sequence of passes and, with a bit of luck and momentum, they will make it over the try line and score. A good position to watch the game from, but bring warm clothing and a thermos flask.

12. INSIDE CENTRE

This player is positioned closest to the fly half and is very occasionally lucky enough to receive a pass. Will inevitably fancy himself as the impact player of the side, ready to make blistering runs through the opposition. Will, however, also need to spend a lot of time tackling. A role that requires pace, strength and patience.

13. OUTSIDE CENTRE

A bit like the inside centre, perhaps a bit smaller, faster and less likely to see the ball.

15. FULL BACK

The last line of defence, usually found hanging back from the rest of the backs. Needs to be able to catch a high ball kicked and, if he can't, then the ball will be kicked towards him for the whole game. In a position to make heroic, try-preventing tackles, saving the embarrassment of the centre who allowed the opposition through the lines. A good home for the more experienced player who will want to pace himself throughout the game for perhaps one long run with the ball.

As you can see, in rugby there is a role for everyone, large and small, old and young. Even if you're a little 'special' and can't quite get your head around all the complicated laws of the game, well, you could always become a referee.

COLLECTIVE TERMS FOR POSITIONS

Props and hooker	Front row
Both locks	Second row
Front row and second row combined	Tight or front five
The flankers and the number 8	Back row, loose forwards or 'loosies'
The forwards	Pack
Scrum half and fly half	Halfbacks
Wingers and centres	Three-quarters
Wingers and full back	Back three
Backs generally	The girls

If I had been a winger, I might have been daydreaming and thinking about how to keep my kit clean for next week.

Bill Beaumont

It takes two hours to get ready, shave my legs and face, moisturise, put fake tan on and do my hair – which takes a bit of time.

Gavin Henson – Welsh back

WHO'S THAT PLAYER?

Identifying and recognising players all adds to the spectators' enjoyment of the game. Rugby naturally helps by supplying players of a wide variety of shapes and sizes, unlike the clones in football and other sports. Shirt numbers linked to positions are still used, unlike the inflationary squad numbers used in the so-called 'beautiful game'.

It was not always as simple. The first international match to introduce numbered shirts is thought to be the Wales v New Zealand clash of 1905. The Scots were the last to adopt the practice of identifying players on their shirts but there was no common approach even then. Some started with the full back as number 1 and worked up from there to the forwards. Others started with the scrum half and worked backwards from there. Some teams omitted the number 13. It was only in 1967 that the International Rugby Board legislated for the numbering system in use today.

Meanwhile, local clubs were allowed to use whatever system they preferred. Bristol and Leicester used letters instead of numbers although, naturally, they too used different systems. Bristol went from A to O starting with the full back, whereas Leicester used the same letters but in the opposite direction. The two teams met in the John Player Cup final in 1983 for a giant game of rugby Scrabble™. Bristol won by 28 points to 22 but narrowly missed getting a triple-word score.

LEAGUE OF GENTLEMEN

League is much, much more physical
than Union, and that's before
anyone starts breaking the rules.

Adrian Hadley (1988)

A TALE OF TWO CODES

As the game of rugby grew it took particular hold in the northern counties of Yorkshire and Lancashire. Large paying crowds were attracted to games and the Yorkshire Cup became a major event. Working-class players, though drawn to the game, were prevented from benefiting financially from the popularity of the sport, which was kept strictly amateur.

This was all very well, but players who were injured, or had to miss work to play or train, would have their wages stopped. A motion to permit a modest payment for players was proposed but at a meeting in London, the Rugby Football Union (RFU), which was dominated by Southern teams filled with wealthier 'Gentleman' players, voted down the proposal and began to suspend Northern clubs and their members. Any rugby union players who dared to play the league version of the game, played with someone who had played the league game, or possibly even opted for a slice of black pudding with their breakfast, would be sanctioned or blackballed.

In August 1895, twenty-one clubs met in the George Hotel in Huddersfield and formed the breakaway Northern Rugby Football Union, specifically to permit payment to players to compensate them for their loss of earnings. The RFU introduced sanctions against any clubs that played against these new breakaway sides. As a result, some amateur Northern teams began to affiliate instead to the new Northern Union.

In 1901 the Lancashire and Yorkshire wings of the Northern Rugby Football Union formed the Northern Rugby League. This led to the name 'rugby league' being given to the new version of the game, which quickly developed its own laws, tactics and character. It remained strongest in the north of England and little known or understood in the South until an actor, John Noakes, was smuggled out of Halifax and into the BBC *Blue Peter* studios sometime in the 1970s. On his own series *Go With Noakes*, he introduced the Home Counties to rugby league, rolling around in the mud with the policemen and engineers that made up Castleford Rugby League Club.

On Thursday night, a meeting of the representatives of the Senior Clubs of Lancashire and Yorkshire was held at the George Hotel, Huddersfield, to consider the question of the formation of a northern Football Union. The meeting was held in private and lasted close on three hours... The first resolution adopted was: 'The clubs here represented decide to form a Northern Rugby Football Union, and pledge themselves to push forward without delay its establishment on the principle of payment for bona fide broken time only.'

Huddersfield Examiner, 30 August 1895

DIFFERENCES BETWEEN
LEAGUE AND UNION

	LEAGUE	UNION
Players per side	Thirteen	Fifteen
After a tackle	Tackled player allowed to get up and heel the ball back to a teammate to restart the game. Each team gets to play for a set of six tackles before handing over possession.	Tackler has to roll away but other players can compete for the ball. A ruck or a maul often forms around the tackled player.
Scrums	Two packs of six players each – no real pushing and the side putting the ball in always gets possession of the ball.	Two packs of eight players – both sides push and compete for the ball.

	LEAGUE	UNION
Ball goes into touch	Restart with a scrum.	Restart with a line-out.
Points for a try	Four	Five
Points for a drop goal	One	Three
Points for a penalty	Two	Three
UK season	September to April	February to September
Before satellite broadcasting took over everything, traditionally played on a...	Saturday afternoon	Sunday afternoon
Popular first names for players	Sebastian, Jules and Tarquin	Josh, Gethin and Lee

The main difference between
playing league and union is
that now I get my hangovers on
Monday instead of Sunday.

Tom David, Welsh league and union international

It's the first time I've been cold
for seven years. I was never cold
playing rugby league.

Jonathan Davies on returning to the union code

FAMOUS PLAYERS WHO HAVE PLAYED BOTH CODES

JONATHAN DAVIES represented Wales in both rugby union and league. He left school at seventeen, became an apprentice painter and decorator, and started playing for Neath in 1982. His first union cap for Wales was against England in 1985 when he was named Man of the Match.

After disputes with the Welsh union authorities he signed for league side Widnes in 1998 for the princely sum of £225,000. After bulking up, and a summer spell in Australia, he made it into the Welsh and the Great Britain national rugby league sides, playing in his last league test in 1995.

Davies returned to Wales to be closer to his family. He also returned to the rugby union family, which had just turned professional. He signed for Cardiff, where he played until 1997. He is now much in demand as a media commentator for both rugby league and union coverage.

JASON ROBINSON was one of the first batch of players to make the shift from league to union when the latter turned professional. Nicknamed 'Billy Whizz', he made his name in the Wigan rugby league Challenge Cup-winning side of 1993. He played on the wing for the Great Britain side against New Zealand aged just nineteen.

As rugby league moved to become a summer sport, Robinson opted for a few games with newly professional union side Bath in the 1996 season. He continued playing league during the warmer months of the year.

In 2000, he moved to union full time, signing for Sale Sharks and working his way into the England national team by February of the following year. He played in fifty-six internationals and scored thirty tries, including a memorable one in England's World Cup final victory against Australia in 2003.

He played his last international against South Africa in the World Cup final of 2007. He became head coach for Sale in 2009 but the stresses and strains of running a Premiership side didn't seem to suit him. A year later he came out of retirement to play for the National Two North side Fylde, who, oddly enough, won the league that year.

I'm forty-nine, I've had a brain
haemorrhage and a triple bypass
and I could still go out and play a
reasonable game of rugby union.
But I wouldn't last thirty seconds
in rugby league.

Graham Lowe (1995)

QUESTIONS IN THE HOUSE: 27 FEBRUARY 1995

DOUG HOYLE MP FOR WARRINGTON NORTH: Is the Minister aware of the case of my constituent, Adrian Spencer, who played amateur rugby league football with Woolston? He played a few games for London Crusaders, for which he received no payment; yet when he played in the Varsity match he was suspended for 12 months. Will the Minister note the contrast between him and Mike Catt, the England player, who admitted receiving £140 per week expenses when he played in South Africa but was exonerated?

Will he seek a meeting with the Rugby Union to condemn the injustice to my constituent and ask for his reinstatement forthwith? Will he also ask it to apply rules for 1995 and not those more akin to 1895?

IAIN SPROAT, PARLIAMENTARY UNDER-SECRETARY OF STATE FOR NATIONAL HERITAGE: The hon. Gentleman makes an important point about Adrian Spencer, who played for only a few minutes; he was on and off the field so quickly that I hardly noticed him, but the hon. Gentleman's point is none the less important and I will draw it to the attention of the rugby union authorities.

Rugby union fiercely guarded its amateur status for almost one hundred years after the split with rugby league. The chaps in charge, with their blazers and club ties, clung on to the tradition and fended off those vulgar types who wanted to make money from their beloved sport. The English class system kept rugby untainted by filthy lucre so only people who already had lots of cash could afford the time and opportunities to play at the highest levels.

The pressure to pay players didn't go away. With the huge physical and time demands on players, many were tempted to switch codes to make a living from the game. As attendances grew and more money came into the game, clubs tried to find ways round the rules to prevent their players from defecting to the Northern professional sides. Welsh clubs developed the practice of 'boot money' as cash was put into players' footwear whilst they were cleaned after a game. The National Heritage Committee of the House of Commons issued a report condemning 'shamateurism' and claiming that the amateur status of rugby union was no more than a veil.

With media moguls looking at the game, the pressure grew and in August 1995 the International Rugby Board declared that the game would become professional. Although players welcomed the relaxation of the rules, the game's administrators, particularly in England, were ill prepared. A later parliamentary report in 1999 found that, 'The structure of rugby union has moved uneasily from its ancestral Corinthian amateur past to its modern professional status.' No professional rugby union club in England was making an operational profit and clubs complained that players' wages were spiralling out of control.

I'm still an amateur, of course, but
I became rugby's first millionaire
five years ago.

David Campese

I couldn't afford to.

Welsh international Barry John when asked why he
hadn't switched to professional rugby league from the
apparently amateur union game

FIFTY-SEVEN OLD FARTS

In 1995 England captain Will Carling was sacked for failing to show sufficient reverence to the sport's administrators in an interview for the Channel Four documentary *Fair Game* when he said, 'If the game is run properly as a professional game, you do not need fifty-seven old farts running rugby.' He was reacting to accusations from the RFU secretary accusing players of cheating for trying to get round the rules.

RFU secretary Dudley Wood described it as 'a very sad day for English rugby' and said that Carling's position as captain had become untenable and the committee had no alternative but to dismiss him.

Carling was one of the most successful ever England skippers, having won back-to-back Grand Slams in the Six Nations tournaments of 1991 and 1992 and again in 1995. After an outcry from players and fans, he was quickly reinstated and went on to lead the team to the World Cup semi-finals in South Africa.

FACTS AND FIGURES

Grandmother or tails, sir?

Anon rugby referee to Princess Anne's son Peter
Phillips, Gordonstoun School's rugby captain, for his
pre-match coin-toss preference (1995)

OLDEST PLAYER IN THE WORLD

In 2005 Sadayoshi Morita of Japan was declared the world's oldest rugby player at the age of ninety. Having played the game since 1934, when the game was still very new in Japan, he had been in training three times a week for seventy years and had no plans to stop. 'It is extraordinarily tough for a ninety-year-old guy to run at top speed,' he told *The Guardian*. 'But you must get over it to enjoy playing rugby. If it weren't for the sprints in this game, I would be able to play rugby until I was 110 years old.'

YOUNGEST PLAYER IN AN INTERNATIONAL

Many of the greatest players start young. Jonah Lomu was the youngest All Black, getting his first cap aged 19 years and 45 days. Mathew Tait made his England debut the day before his nineteenth birthday. Jonny Wilkinson first ran out in an England shirt aged 18 years and 314 days. One of the earliest record holders for precocious international rugby playing was Henri Laird, who played for England aged 18 years and 134 days in 1927.

The current record is held by Tom Prydie, who made his debut for Wales against Italy on Saturday, 20 March 2010, aged 18 years and 25 days. Earlier that year Prydie, still aged seventeen, had been a surprise inclusion in the thirty-five-man Welsh Six Nations squad, despite playing just two starts and only one hundred and sixty-seven minutes of professional senior rugby for the Ospreys side. Notified by a text message from Welsh coach Warren Gatland just twenty minutes before the news was made public, he thought at first that it was a practical joke.

TALLEST PLAYER

Scottish international Richard Metcalfe, at 7 feet 0 inches, is the tallest rugby player recorded. Playing in the second row, unsurprisingly he had a distinct edge over other players in the line-out. However, in open play his higher centre of gravity meant that his body position in contact situations was far from ideal. He made his debut in Scotland's victory over England in the first round of the Six Nations tournament in 2000 and went on to gain eleven caps. Sadly he was forced out of the game in 2003 by a long-term knee injury, presumably caused by being headbutted by scrum halves one too many times.

I may not have been very tall or very athletic, but the one thing I did have was the most effective backside in world rugby.

Jim Glennon (1991)

GREATEST TRY OF ALL TIME: GARETH EDWARDS, BARBARIANS V ALL BLACKS 1973

When the Baa-Baas lined up at Cardiff Arms Park against an All Black side that had been touring for three months, the feeling in the traditionally under-prepared, celebrity-packed invitation side was one of nervous anticipation. 'We went on the field determined to try to win the game but petrified that we might get run over,' said Wales and British Lions fly half Gareth Edwards.

After just a few minutes of frantic kicking and a series of unpunished high tackles, Phil Bennett caught a New Zealand kick a few yards from his own try line. Rather than kicking for touch and giving his teammates a much-needed breather, he sidestepped three All Blacks and began the sequence that led to one of rugby's greatest ever moments.

The ball passed through the hands of some of the legendary players of the time – J. P. R. Williams and on to Derek Quinnell, whose burst of speed made the try possible. Edwards, the scrum half, arrived at full speed at the perfect moment and set off outside the remaining New Zealand defenders to score in the left corner.

BBC commentator Cliff Morgan captured the moment perfectly: 'This is Gareth Edwards, a dramatic start, what a score. Oooh that fellow Edwards...' and, when he'd caught his breath, continued, 'If the greatest writer of the written word would have written that story, no one would have believed it. That really was something.'

The final score was Barbarians 23 All Blacks 11.

INTERNATIONAL RUGBY RANKINGS

There are ninety-four rugby-playing nations today regulated and ranked by the International Rugby Board. The rankings are based on a points exchange system – if one side loses points, the team that beats it gains the same amount.

Ranking points are awarded based on the scale of a victory. If a team wins a fixture by a margin of greater than fifteen, more ranking points are exchanged. Ranking points are doubled during the World Cup, reflecting the added importance of these games.

England briefly topped the rankings when they were introduced in 2003. Since then they have been dominated by New Zealand's All Blacks, with the Springboks of South Africa taking an occasional turn at the top.

A WORLD IN UNION

Rugby is, of course, not just about the national sides. It is about local clubs and their players and supporters. So, here are the top ten rugby nations, but ranked in order of how many registered players they have according to the International Rugby Board:

1. England   2,549,196 players in 2,099 clubs
2. South Africa   632,184 players in 1,453 clubs
3. France   313,877 players in 1,630 clubs
4. Ireland   153,080 players in 221 clubs
5. New Zealand   137,835 players in 562 clubs
6. Australia   86,953 players in 787 clubs
7. Italy   66,176 players in 784 clubs
8. Wales   50,557 players in 239 clubs
9. Scotland   38,500 players in 251 clubs
10. Fiji   36,030 players in 490 clubs

After a pile of players extricated themselves from a ruck, a young back was left lying on the ground, clutching his nether regions.

The physio ran onto the field with the first aid kit and the magic sponge. As he attempted to treat the injured player who was writhing on the ground in agony, the fly half moaned, 'For God's sake, don't rub them! Just count them!'

WORLD'S WORST INTERNATIONAL RUGBY SIDE

Finland sits at the bottom of the world rankings and has done for some years. They played their first international in 1982, losing at home to Switzerland by sixty points to nil. They did beat Estonia in 2010 by fifty-five points to five, but their worst defeat to date was being beaten 100–0 in Denmark in 1987.

There are just twelve clubs affiliated to the governing body in Finland, including the Santa Claus club, who play in Rovaniemi, Lapland, on the edge of the Arctic Circle. Given the long, frozen winters, it's no surprise that the domestic rugby season starts only in May when the ground has thawed and most other Northern Hemisphere nations' seasons have finished playing for the year. No one seems to have quite worked out how to bring the game indoors, which might help the Arctic nations climb the world rankings.

CLUB COMPETITIONS

It took just over a hundred years for the Rugby Football Union to sanction a formal competition between more than two sides. Up until the early 1970s it had argued that leagues and knockout competitions were not in the best interests of the game.

However, in 1972 they launched an RFU cup competition for senior sides, bringing together some sides which had never previously played each other. That became the John Player Cup and through various sponsors has now morphed into the LV= Cup (see below).

Given the complex system of bonus points, play-offs and convoluted promotion and relegation regulations, those early administrators might have had a point.

AVIVA PREMIERSHIP
(PREVIOUSLY SPONSORED BY GUINNESS, ZURICH, ALLIED DUNBAR AND COURAGE)

- League for the top twelve clubs in England.

- Teams play each other home and away.

- Four points for a win, two points for a draw.

- One bonus point for losing a match by seven points or fewer.

- One bonus point for scoring four or more tries in a game.

- The top four clubs qualify automatically for the Heineken Cup (see below).

- The top four clubs also enter a set of finals. Teams 1 and 4 play in one semi-final and teams 2 and 3 play in another, the higher side having home advantage. The winners play in a final at Twickenham and the winner of that is then, and only then, crowned champions.

- The last-place club is relegated to the RFU Championship (formerly National Division One).

MAGNERS LEAGUE
(ORIGINALLY KNOWN AS THE CELTIC LEAGUE)

- League for twelve sides from Wales, Ireland, Scotland, France and Italy.

- Points and bonuses are awarded along the same lines as the Aviva Premiership and the top four clubs go into a similar set of play-offs.

- The top-placed side in the league gets to choose the venue for the final.

ANGLO-WELSH CUP
(CURRENTLY KNOWN AS THE LV-CUP)

- Knockout competition between the English Premiership sides and the four Welsh sides in the Magners League.

- Teams start off in four pools of four teams with one Welsh side in each pool.

- The winners then play each other in semi-finals and then a final.

- The winners, if they are an English side, then get to qualify for the Heineken Cup.

HEINEKEN CUP

- Competition for twenty-four clubs from England (six teams), France (six), Wales (three), Scotland (two), Ireland (three) and Italy (two). The twenty-third and twenty-fourth Heineken Cup places go to the nation or nations of the previous year's Heineken Cup and Amlin Challenge Cup winners. England and France are capped on a maximum of seven teams each.

- Teams start in six pools of four.

- Pool winners and the next two best-placed runners-up enter into a knockout stage.

- The final is played at one of the six nations' national stadiums.

EUROPEAN CHALLENGE CUP
(CURRENTLY SPONSORED BY AMLIN)

- Competition for European clubs not in the Heineken Cup, including those who drop out at the pool stage.

- Twenty teams in five pools of four.

- The winners and the three best runners-up go into a set of quarter-finals and work their way towards a final.

- The winner then qualifies for the Heineken Cup the following season, unless they are from England or France and that nation has already reached its quota of teams by other means, or if there is an 'r' in the month, possibly.

THE DARK ARTS –
FORWARD TECHNIQUE

Despite what a lot of people might think, it's actually quite fun in there.

Jeff Probyn, England prop, on the dark arts of
playing in the front row

SCRUMMAGING

For many forwards, scrums are the whole point of rugby: the set piece where eight forwards from each side pack down and attempt to push each other over the ball. Out of the sight of spectators, referees and backs, great battles are fought between individuals and teams.

It is also one of the most dangerous areas of the game and over the years great efforts have been made to try and keep it safer. It remains the point of the game most likely to result in a serious neck injury. Referees, especially in the junior levels of the game, need to take great care to control the scrum and make sure that the two packs and the fronts in particular are reasonably evenly matched and can cope with the pressure.

A scrum is called when someone knocks the ball on. 'Knocking the ball on' is another way of saying 'dropping the ball'. It is quite possible that your first impact on the game as someone flings a wild pass towards you will be to trigger a scrum by failing to catch the ball and knocking it forward instead. (If by some chance the ball goes backwards after hitting you, you will be spared the embarrassment.)

Scrums are also triggered by a forward pass, or when there is a general pile-up over the ball and the referee wants to find a slightly more civilised way of restarting the game.

If a scrum is given against your side, the other side will have the advantage of putting the ball in. This means that they are more likely, but not certain, to retrieve the ball from the back of the scrum on their side as a result.

CROUCH, TOUCH, PAUSE, ENGAGE

In 2007 referees introduced a four-step process to initiating a scrum. Once the pack is bound together and the ball is ready, the referee will call out in turn:

- 'Crouch' – The front row drop down into a sumo squat-type position ready for contact.

- 'Touch' – The props on either side reach out and tap their opposite number with their free, outside hand. This stage was introduced to make sure the two front rows are a safe distance from each other, and to reduce the power of the initial hit.

- 'Pause' – Both packs brace themselves for impact.

- 'Engage' – The bulk of the force comes from the second row as they straighten out their legs, pushing the props forward as they interlock their heads.

Both sides are meant to hold their shove until the ball is put in the middle. They then try to push the other pack back as the hookers attempt to heel the ball back to their side.

WINNING ONE AGAINST THE HEAD

Front-row players are sometimes unfairly thought to be a little slow mentally as well as physically. They may be accused, for example, of having a little trouble keeping track of the score throughout the game. However, one score they will keep track of is the number of scrums won against the head. That is when the ball is put in by the opposition scrum half and yet between them they manage to retrieve it to their side.

At the professional level of the game it is very rare to see scrums won against the head. Scrum halves and hookers have a well-timed routine which is almost impossible to disrupt unless the props are having a really bad day. Even in the amateur levels of the sport it is comparatively uncommon. More than a handful of victories against the head in any game is unlikely.

One of the greatest displays of hooking was during the French tour of South Africa in 1964. In the opening fixture against Rhodesia, the French hooker Jean-Michel Cabanier came up against the Springbok veteran Ronnie Hill. Hill won an impressive ten scrums against the head. Although the French won the game 34–11, the Gallic front row will have been hanging their heads in shame. Cabanier was left out of the test pack for the only full international fixture of the tour.

MAULS AND RUCKS –
MAKING SENSE OF IT ALL

Maul: when someone is tackled, but manages to stay on his feet, a maul often is the result. Supporting players from both sides get stuck in grabbing hold of whatever they can, pushing the pack forwards whilst attempting to manoeuvre the ball to the back of the maul for the next attack.

If the tackled player goes down to the ground with the ball, it becomes a **ruck**. The forwards' job is the same but the rules have now changed. You are no longer allowed to touch the ball with your hands and have to use your feet to move the ball back to your scrum half.

Colin Meads is the kind of player you expect to see emerging from a ruck with the remains of a jockstrap between his teeth.

Tom O'Reilly

Though it is lawful to hold any
players in a maul, this holding does
not include attempts to throttle or
strangle, which are totally opposed
to all the principles of the game.

Edinburgh Academical FC rules (1858)

WHO NEEDS BACKS ANYWAY?

As Welsh captain Clive Rowlands settled down in his hotel room on the eve of the 1963 fixture against Scotland at Murrayfield, he totted up the weights of the two packs in the published match day programme. The packs due to meet the next day were apparently roughly equal in weight, with Wales having a slight advantage of just a few pounds.

The next morning, Rowlands checked the weights of his forwards and discovered that the programme had considerably understated the figures of two of his back-row forwards. He would be taking to the field with a Welsh pack weighing roughly two stones more than the Scots.

Rowlands saw an opportunity to beat the Scots at their home fortress for the first time in a decade. Playing at scrum half, he completely ignored his backs for the entire game, kicking the ball into touch at every opportunity for a total of 111 line-outs, a record for an international. Wales spent most of the game deep in the Scottish half and eventually ground out an unattractive but, for Clive Rowlands, deeply satisfying win.

The IRB were less impressed and swiftly changed the laws, making it illegal to kick directly into touch unless you were behind your own 25-yard line (now 22-metre line).

LINE-OUT CALLS

These coded calls are used to communicate where the hooker will endeavour to throw the ball, and what is supposed to happen next, without letting the defending side know.

Three-word codes are often used, and the three words chosen don't share any letters – e.g. THAMES ROWING CLUB. The first word signifies the front of the line-out, the second the middle and so on. The line-out caller will then think of a word that begins with one of the letters in the chosen word for where he wants the ball thrown e.g. for a front ball the caller might shout a word beginning with the letters in THAMES – Tiramisu, Hernia, Algernon, Manchester, Easter or Sausages.

Other calls are then added to suggest what the catcher might want to try and do with the ball. In theory he will have the following choices: catch the ball, drop gently to the ground, gather his fellow forwards around him and drive down the pitch in a maul formation – a 'catch and drive'; he might alternatively try and pass the ball to the scrum half whilst he is still supported high in the air – this generates a quick ball for the backs to run off with and is useful if the other pack is generally more dominant – an 'off the top'. Other calls might be used for a specific one-off line-out move – typically one that will only be used once or twice in a game.

All of this rather depends on having a relatively lucid pack. All too often, elaborate systems of calls and codes fall apart as a set of dazed and bewildered forwards trudge towards the try line after a brutal first few minutes of the game, only to find that they have no memory whatsoever of the calls agreed before the match.

Signals ambiguity should be avoided. A word sign with the letter P was the signal for the forwards to go right. When predictably, Gareth Edwards called 'psychology' half the forwards went left.

Carwyn James, coach of the Lions tour of New Zealand (1971)

MIND OVER MATTER

I don't know about us not having
a Plan B when things went wrong,
we looked like we didn't have a
Plan A.

Geoff Cooke, after England had been humbled by New
Zealand in a World Cup semi-final (1995)

JONNY, THE BUDDHA AND SCHRÖDINGER'S CAT

When Jonny Wilkinson returned to rugby in 2008 after a bout of injury he arrived with a new mop of wavy golden hair. He was also sporting a new understanding of quantum physics, a rudimentary grasp of Buddhism and an unfamiliar smile.

The England fly half claimed in an interview with *The Times* to have come to see the world in an entirely new light, free from his worries about life, death and rugby.

In spite of the success and fame that had followed his last-minute drop goal to secure England's world cup victory in Australia in 2003, Wilkinson was a tortured soul. He struggled with endless injuries as he pushed himself to the limit in every game. In his anguish, he began reading about quantum physics and came across the phenomenon known as Schrödinger's Cat.

Austrian physicist Erwin Schrödinger used the fictitious feline to explain a problem at the heart of quantum physics. Apparently some subatomic particles exist in two states, but the act of measuring them effectively forces them into one particular state. He sought to illustrate this by imagining a cat in a sealed box rigged in such a way that there was a 50/50 chance that the poor animal would have died. Cruel, but don't worry, it's only an imaginary cat. Before the box is opened, according to quantum physics, the cat is both alive and dead. As soon as one opens the box, the cat is either alive or dead. Observing it has made it so.

This apparently had a huge effect on the young Wilkinson, who said, 'The idea that an observer can change the world just by looking at it... it hit me like a steam train.' He concluded that his own way of thinking about things was influencing the way they turned out. He found Buddhism helped him overcome his fear of failure and then he grew his hair a bit – as you do.

Whether it improved his rugby, or lengthened his playing career as well as his hair, is anyone's guess. However, it did seem to stop him looking so stressed and miserable all the time and that can't be bad for an Austrian physicist's imaginary moggie.

Don't ask me about emotions in the Welsh dressing room. I'm someone who cries when he watches *Little House on the Prairie.*

Former Welsh second row Bob Norster

A TIME TO DANCE

The performance of the Maori traditional dance, known as the haka, by the New Zealand rugby team dates back to 1888. This curtain-raiser to every one of the All Black's fixtures ever since requires players to learn an intimidating sequence of foot stamping, finger wiggling and somewhat bizarre facial expressions. Along with its warlike chanting, it has been a perennial favourite with the crowds ever since its introduction. Opposition sides try to observe the ritual with a respectful but suitably menacing look.

Fortunately, English sides have so far resisted the temptation to respond with a morris dance complete with ankle bells and hankies.

Although various hakas have been used over the years, the best known is 'Ka Mate', celebrating the victory of life over death. Its words translate as:

I die! I die! I live! I live!
I die! I die! I live! I live!
This is the hairy man
Who fetched the Sun
And caused it to shine again
One upward step!
Another upward step!
An upward step, another... the Sun shines!

Hakas have also been adopted by the teams of Fiji, Tonga and Samoa, as well as many US school and college American football teams – though next to most end-zone dances the haka seems quite normal!

IMAGERY

Some of the great players of the game use visual imagery to help them perform at the highest level. England kicking legend Jonny Wilkinson famously visualises kicking the ball straight into the arms of an imaginary woman called Doris sitting twenty rows behind the posts.

According to sports psychologists Bruce Howe and Bruce Hale, mental imagery helps a player rehearse strategies, retain focus and make split-second decisions during a match.

Successful imagery has four principles: relaxation, realism, regularity and reinforcement. Players might use a deep-breathing exercise to relax and then use all their senses to create a vivid image so the scene in their mind is as realistic as an actual match. For many professionals, mental imagery is part of their regular pre-match routine and will be scheduled into their weekly training programme. They will use video clips from games to reinforce and strengthen the mental images.

Imagery can work well for novice players too. With regular practice it can bring real improvements to your game, or indeed to your post-match drinking challenges.

Subdue and penetrate.

The motto of the All Blacks

The whole point of rugby is that it is, first and foremost, a state of mind, a spirit.

Jean-Pierre Rives, French rugby player

Look what these bastards have done to Wales. They've taken our coal, our water, our steel. They buy our houses and they only live in them for a fortnight every twelve months. What have they given us? Absolutely nothing. We've been exploited, raped, controlled and punished by the English – and that's who you are playing this afternoon.

Phil Bennett, Welsh Captain, team talk – Cardiff 1977 (Wales won 14–9 with J. P. R Williams and Gareth Edwards scoring a try each)

BACKS TO THE FUTURE

I've seen a lot of people like him,
but they weren't playing
on the wing.

Colin Meads on Jonah Lomu

PASSING

Passing is really the preserve of the backs, who relish their ability to spin the ball, with a smart flick of their wrists, in a fast straight line into the hands of a fellow back several metres away. In theory, the faster and further they can successfully pass it, the more chance the team has in finding a gap they can run through and score a try.

The best passer in the team is quite often the scrum half, whose basic purpose is to get the ball to the fly half, at the right moment, as quickly and accurately as possible. A fly half would ideally like to be able to stand a nice safe distance away from the forwards, so that when he gets the ball he has lots of time and space to decide what to do with it. If the scrum half can pass the ball well, he will make the fly half look good. If he can't, he risks giving the opposition the chance to batter the fly half, steal the ball or both.

Sometimes, under pressure, a scrum half will use a dive pass, where he uses his entire body, unfolding and stretching out to fling the ball, using power from every possible muscle in his tiny little body, to get the ball away from trouble.

PHYSICS OF THE SPIN PASS

A rugby ball thrown as a pass has inertia; that is, the tendency of an object in motion to remain in motion. It will also have some gravity working on it, which pulls the ball down, and there will be some air resistance, which slows the ball down. The scrum half must supply sufficient forward momentum to the ball (through the motions of his arms and body) to counteract the gravity and air resistance in order to accurately deliver it into the hands of his fellow halfback.

Aerodynamics then comes into the mix. The ball will cut through the air more swiftly if it can go pointy end first all the way to its target. To stay in that position it helps if it is spinning about its long axis – the axis that is pointing in the direction the ball is being thrown. As a scrum half passes the rugby ball, he will try to add a spin onto the ball using a flick of his fingers, thumbs and wrist. The ball's angular momentum (movement due to rotation around an axis, a product of mass and angular velocity) points in the direction of its long axis. At the same time, torque, the force that causes twisting and turning due to air drag, is pointing at right angles to the angular momentum. As the ball travels on its semi-parabolic arc, this wind torque produces a small change in the ball's angular momentum, which allows the ball to continue to rotate around its trajectory. Spinning stabilizes the ball through angular momentum and torque, allowing it to continue to travel in a tight spiral.

When thrown in this way, the ball offers the smallest possible cross-sectional area against the oncoming air, which causes the minimal amount of aerodynamic drag. If the ball does not spin properly, air travels excessively under its tip as it falls, causing it to tumble and lose some of its forward momentum due to a greater cross-sectional area being exposed to the wind. However, when the scrum half does throw a pass with a decent amount of spin, the ball will travel fast and flat into the arms of a grateful fly half.

OTHER SORTS OF PASS

- Pop pass – a short, gentle pass, where the ball is 'popped' up a foot or two and caught, ideally, at the top of its arc.

- Dummy pass – a pretend pass, where the player goes through all the motions of the pass without actually releasing the ball. This is designed to distract an opposing defender into heading off to where the ball was going to be passed, rather than tackling the player with the ball. With luck, this then creates a gap for the attacking player to run through.

- Hospital pass – a badly delivered pass, possibly one wafted high in the air, that takes so long to reach its intended recipient that it arrives at the same time as a rampaging opposition forward. The recipient reaches up to catch the ball at the same time as the tackler clatters into his chest, often breaking one or more ribs in the process.

- Khyber Pass – a mountain path linking Pakistan and Afghanistan, 3,500 feet above sea level.

FAMOUS PLAYER: JONAH LOMU

Jonah Lomu, one of the world's first international rugby icons, and possibly the greatest ever back, was raised in Tonga for the first six years of his life. He had a turbulent childhood and left home at fourteen, when he had finally had enough of his violent and alcoholic father.

At 19 years and 45 days old he became the youngest All Black ever, winning his first cap against France in 1994. But it was in the 1995 World Cup that he really made his mark, scoring seven tries in five games. He introduced the international audience to his 'Maori sidestep', which is where a player from the Pacific Island nation runs in a completely straight line, using his additional weight and momentum to blast away any player in his path. Lomu used this famously as he ran through England's full back Mike Catt to score one of his four tries against England in the semi-final.

What people didn't know at the time was that he was suffering from a severe kidney disorder throughout the tournament and spent most of the time between matches recovering in bed. He

had a kidney transplant in 2004, with the replacement kidney being donated by New Zealand radio host Grant Kereama.

He played sixty-three times for his country between 1994 and 2002, scoring 185 points in total. His pace, power and reputation intimidated opposition defenders. If he wasn't scoring tries himself, his mere presence would create defensive gaps for his teammates to exploit.

Interviewed in *The Daily Telegraph*, he said, 'When I play at my peak I get into a different zone. I become a completely different person. I can't really explain it.

It's almost like you're running, but you're watching yourself while you're running – like an out-of-body experience. I do what I've got to do to get to where I need to get. You do see Mike Catt in front of you… but that's what rugby is all about. If someone is in front of you and you have to go over the top of them, that's the way the game goes.'

After a few attempted comebacks, injury setbacks and a brief diversion into bodybuilding, Lomu ended up in France playing for the semi-professional side Marseille Vitrolles. He continues to be an ambassador for the game.

BACKS MOVES

LOOP – This is a very basic move that is regularly practised on the training ground. After passing down the line, the passer loops back round the player who has received the ball. This adds one more player to the line and a potential overlap.

SWITCH – Instead of the ball being passed down the line, the passer drifts out along the defensive line as one of the other backs runs back towards him and catches the ball, switching the direction of play by heading back in towards the forwards. This creates a little confusion in the opposition line as they try and work out who to track.

DUMMY SWITCH – In this play the back running in to receive the switch pass typically makes a bit more noise but doesn't get the ball. He hopes that more defenders will track him, thereby creating a gap somewhere else further down the line.

KICKING

To kick or not to kick – that is often the question, and one that demands an answer very quickly indeed. Many a spectator would rather you didn't. Watching an endless exchange of high kicks between opposing full backs is hardly worth paying the admission price for. However, exhausted defenders will always welcome a well-placed kick into touch to get the ball a decent distance away from the try line.

Kicking is usually the preserve of one or two experienced backs in any side, whether professional or amateur. Designated kickers can usually be identified by their spotlessly clean shirts and elegantly coiffured hairdos. For all the touchline criticism and on-field complaints they might receive, a skilled kicker in any side can make the difference between winning and losing.

DROP KICK – Used to restart the game and to score heroic drop goals. The ball has to bounce on the ground before it is struck with the boot.

PUNT – Used in open play and from free kicks and as an option for penalties. Often used to kick the ball into touch when a side is defending within its own 22-metre line. If the ball is kicked directly into touch from outside the '22', the resulting line-out is taken from a point parallel with where the ball was kicked rather than where it left the field.

GRUBBER – A kick from hand is designed to bobble awkwardly along the ground for your teammates to chase after as the defending side wonders which way it is going to bounce. Looks like the sort of kick that was invented by mistake as someone mistimed a kick into touch.

UP-AND-UNDER – A kick lofted high enough and far enough for the kicker to chase after and win from the opposing defender before it hits the ground. A catchphrase of 1970s rugby league commentator Eddie Waring. Also known as a 'garryowen' after the Limerick rugby union club that popularised the technique.

BOX KICK – A tight over-the-shoulder kick used by scrum halves in a tight spot, typically trapped behind the base of a scrum. Well placed, it can confuse the opposition. The scrum half aims to put the ball behind the opposition forwards and isolate the opposing wingers or full backs, with his own wingers chasing the ball hard.

CROSS-FIELD KICK – Relies on good communication between the fly half and a winger, and a lucky bounce, but gives an attacking alternative to passing the ball along the backline.

PLACE KICK – Once upon a time, the place kick between the posts was the whole point of the game. Touching the ball down over the try line wasn't rewarded with any points. Instead, all it entitled you to was the opportunity to 'try' and kick the ball between the posts. Nowadays five points are awarded for a try and just two points for a conversion. You can also use a place kick at goal if you win a penalty within your own kicking range. Slot that one home and there are three points on offer.

Goal kicking is a mixture of
technique and temperament.
You must try to box up the goal-
kicking technique in a little
compartment.

Rob Andrew, 1989

MASTERING THE PLACE KICK AT GOAL

- Use a kicking tee to position the ball, pointing towards the goalposts. Failing that, a small pile of sand will do the trick if you happen to have a bucket of sand or a builder's yard handy. Alternatively, make a dent in the ground using your heel with your back to the posts and then mould the mud with your hands.

- Place the ball, tilting it so it is pointing straight towards the goal posts.

- Adjust it slightly to expose the 'sweet spot'. This is the area about a third of the way up the ball where you will get the best connection and distance.

- Stand over the ball in the kicking position to make sure it is in the right place to strike.

- Measure out a run-up, a few paces backwards and maybe one or two to the side. The choice is yours. The routine itself will help you to relax and focus.

- Concentrate on the sweet spot.

- Imagine the ball going straight through the posts.

- Run up to the ball in a smooth curve with your body positioned at 45 degrees.

- Angle your body so that your non-kicking shoulder is side on to the target.

- Place your supporting foot as close to the ball as possible.

- Keep your centre of gravity over the ball.

- Strike the ball on the sweet spot with the instep of your foot.

- Follow through with your toes pointing in the direction of the ball, bringing your leg up high.

- Jog back towards your teammates as you graciously accept their applause and gratitude to you for putting some well-needed points onto the scoreboard.

Tasty Tackles

I like to get one really good
tackle in early in the game,
even if it's late.

Ray Gravell, former Welsh rugby player

Once William Webb Ellis came up with the idea of picking up the ball and running with it, other players needed to think of ways of stopping him. Tackling was the result and is the core skill today for all players of the game, whether league or union.

Tackling can be a little intimidating to learn. Putting your body in the way of someone running at you with a ball and a determined look on their face could be considered the definition of madness. However, with a little technique and practice a successful tackle can be enormously satisfying and surprisingly pain free.

The important thing to remember is that the person with the greatest momentum is likely to come out better from any tackling encounter. Momentum (as anyone who has sat through a physics lesson will know) is equal to mass multiplied by velocity, which is good news for overweight forwards who do not have to run quite as fast to make a successful tackle.

To maximise your momentum, you will need to overcome the instinct to 'stand off' from a tackle, i.e. the instinct to check your speed ever so slightly before the impact. This will take practice, first against tackle bags and then against your fellow teammates on the training pitch.

Every time I went to tackle him,
Horrocks went one way, Taylor
went the other, and all I got was
the bloody hyphen.

Nick England, on trying to catch

Phil Horrocks-Taylor

MASTERING THE TACKLE

- As you approach the player with the ball, set your body so that your shoulders are above the ball carrier's hips and below their ribs.

- Concentrate on your target – the ball carrier's thigh. You are going to try and get your arms round his legs and bring him to the ground.

- Lower yourself into a crouching position and get your shoulder ready to make the initial impact.

- Drive with your legs. This will give you the momentum to make an impact with your shoulder on their thigh.

- Position your head behind your opponent's body. Think 'cheek to cheek' and get the side of your face behind a buttock.

- Wrap your arms around his legs, grip tightly and hang on for dear life.

- Once your opponent falls to the ground, your work is not yet done. Your next objective is to help your side win the ball and avoid giving away a penalty.

- Once tackled and brought to the ground, your opponent must release the ball. You have to roll away and, if you can, get to your feet before playing the ball.

The club chairman visited one of his vets' team players in hospital the day after a big match.

'I understand you were the victim of a late tackle,' said the chairman, putting a bag of grapes on the bedside cabinet.

'You could call it a late tackle, I suppose,' said the player. 'He knocked me out in the bar after the match.'

A TRY-SAVING AND CAREER-MAKING TACKLE

The Bledisloe Cup is awarded to the winner of the annual test fixture between Australia and New Zealand. On 17 August 1994, a dramatic tackle in the last few minutes of the game by a young George Gregan ensured that Australia narrowly saved the match and lifted the trophy that year.

George Gregan had won his first cap earlier in the season against Italy. With full time approaching, New Zealand, trailing 20–16, had one last chance to score. A ruck formed on the left-hand side of the pitch, the ball emerged and found its way to All Black Jeff Wilson. Wilson accelerated from 40 metres out, through two defenders before coming back inside and brushing off a third. When only 5 metres out he made his descent towards the line. The try looked unstoppable.

George Gregan seemed to appear almost from nowhere. He dived across and the impact saw the ball fall from Wilson's grasp, as they were both in the air a few inches above the try line. The tackle turned a little known Aussie scrum half into an international superstar and one of the biggest names in rugby. He went on to win 139 caps for his country, more than any other Australian ever.

WOMEN'S RUGBY

On the pitch, in training, in the gym, we are just rugby players... I'm a rugby player first. Rugby is what I'm about.

Emily Scarratt

Throughout this book I have referred to rugby players as male. This is, of course, both lazy and outdated. Women's rugby is a steadily growing wing of the sport. It is played in exactly the same way, on the same size pitches with exactly the same rules. Careful inspection of the protective layers available might reveal a slightly different distribution of the padding but otherwise it is the same sport. Boys and girls play mini rugby together up until the age of eleven, and many clubs around the country have a successful women's side.

There is a Women's Rugby World Cup and a Six Nations tournament. In 2010, 13,000 supporters watched the World Cup final between England and New Zealand at the Twickenham Stoop (New Zealand won 13–10).

Rugby may have had a pretty chauvinistic image in the past and deserved it. However, nowadays most clubs are a little more enlightened and those that aren't will still see adding a women's side as a way to increase membership, revitalise the club and see more money spent behind the bar. Other incentives linked to grants and funding all encourage traditional clubs to become a little bit more accessible.

In an interview with *The Observer* in March 2011, the leading star of the English women's game, Maggie Alphonsi, identified a change in attitudes following the most recent World Cup. She noticed then for the first time, when people approached her after a game, they would say that it had been a really great game or that she was a really good rugby player. 'The "Woman" bit they used to put in seems to have gone now... It's not women's rugby. It's just rugby.'

THE SECRET RUGBY SISTERHOOD

The early history of women's rugby seems to be shrouded in mystery, as early female players of the game kept their sporting exploits hidden. An attempt to organise a women's tour of New Zealand in 1891 was cancelled after a public outcry. There are stories of women's games being played behind closed doors in France and England in the early 1900s, with women wearing bathing hats to prevent their hair being caught up as they were tackled. Women's charity games were arranged during World War One, and in 1917 Cardiff Ladies beat Newport Ladies 6–0 at Cardiff Arms Park, but in 1920 a rugby league game in Australia between two women's sides caused a clampdown from the game's authorities.

In the 'swinging sixties' attitudes began to change and students in Edinburgh formed the first recorded university women's side in 1962. The WRFU was formed in England in 1983 and gradually the women's game has grown from there.

Everybody thinks we should have moustaches and hairy arses, but in fact you could put us all on the cover of *Vogue.*

Helen Kirk on female rugby teams (1987)

FAMOUS PLAYER: MARGARET ALPHONSI

'Maggie the Machine' is the star player in the England women's rugby set-up. The 5'4" Saracens flanker has over fifty international caps and a reputation for rib-crunching tackles. Born in Lewisham, South London, Alphonsi started playing rugby at fourteen at school in Salisbury. Captain of Saracens, she has won the women's rugby Premiership for four consecutive seasons.

The highlight of her career so far was probably to play in the 2010 World Cup final against New Zealand. The All Blacks have dominated international women's rugby, much like their male counterparts, but England held them to within three points in the closest final yet.

In 2011 Maggie was voted '*The Sunday Times* Sportswoman of the Year' and was the first woman to win the Rugby Union Writers' Club prestigious Pat Marshall Award. In a sport that now has 14,000 regular players in England, Maggie the Machine will be an inspiration for many more.

RUGBY ROMANCE

Wills and Kate aren't the only couple to have found romance in the Scottish university of St Andrews. Nikki and Euan Isles found each other there and it was the addition of rugby that brought a spark to their relationship. In a real life parallel to the film *Bend It Like Beckham*, Nikki was the captain of the women's rugby side and Euan was their coach. It was on a rugby night out in 1999 that they decided to get together and six years later they were married. Speaking to the *Daily Record*, Nikki said, 'I never thought I would meet Mr Right on a rugby pitch... I found the perfect husband.'

Rugby is neither a Man's game nor a Women's game. It is a universal sport that can be enjoyed by anyone with some space and a ball.

Kate Porter, Australian rugby player (2011)

Rugby by Any Other Name

Big hits go in – there's no bodily contact, the wheelchair is reinforced. If you smash someone then it's a great hit. It can get tasty – and that's why we love it.

Steve Palmer, England wheelchair rugby captain, speaking to *The Guardian*

WHEELCHAIR RUGBY

This Paralympic sport was created in 1976 by five Canadian wheelchair athletes. Derived from wheelchair basketball, the game was originally called 'murderball'. It is a full-contact, aggressive sport played on a hardwood court the same size as a basketball court. Players score by carrying the ball over the goal line but their opponents can use their wheelchairs to block and stop them. It is a fast-moving game, as players must pass or bounce the ball within ten seconds. More than twenty-four countries play the sport and it became a full Paralympic sport in Sydney in 2000, with the USA taking home the gold medal.

FAMOUS PLAYER: JOSIE PEARSON

Josie Pearson's first sporting passion was horse riding but in 2003, aged just seventeen, she broke her neck in a car accident, in which her nineteen-year-old boyfriend tragically died. She spent five months in hospital recovering. The year after the accident, inspired by Paralympic athletes in Greece, she began to contemplate getting back into competitive sport.

After trying the wheelchair sprints, she forced her way into the male-dominated sport of wheelchair rugby. One year into a neuroscience degree at Cardiff University, she left to focus on her sporting career.

In Beijing 2008 she made history by becoming the first woman to represent Britain in the sport, playing alongside the men and giving them more than their money's worth as the British team finished in a very respectable fourth place.

'I picked up the basics pretty quickly,' said Josie to her local newspaper, the *Hereford Times*. 'It's an adrenaline sport and a brilliant sport. The guys are welcoming and I never felt singled out just because I am a girl.'

RUGBY SEVENS

This version of the sport is played during the summer, and gives backs a chance to run around after a long season standing around in the cold waiting for the forwards to release the ball. It's played on a full-size pitch, with two halves of just seven minutes each, the scrums consisting of just three players from each side. With fewer players, there is a lot more running around and players very quickly build up a substantial thirst. Sevens festivals seem to involve significantly more drinking than playing.

The Hong Kong Sevens is the premier international competition, played in March every year. Twenty-four teams compete over three days for a prize fund of $150,000. The atmosphere in the South Stand of the Hong Kong Stadium can get very lively, with fancy dress, Mexican waves and the inevitable streakers.

BEACH RUGBY

Hot on the heels of beach volleyball, a new seaside sporting spectacle may be emerging. Starting in 2006, Swansea has hosted an annual beach rugby tournament and in 2010 it attracted thirty teams and a crowd of over 2,500.

With the tide lapping around the touchline, a team calling itself Warriors Rugby narrowly beat the Reservoir Togs in the final in 2010, and thereby qualified to represent Wales at an international competition in Lignano Sabbiadoro, Italy the following year.

There may not be a formal set of internationally agreed regulations yet, but it can't be long before a group of three legally qualified Rugby School alumni will be convened in their bathing suits to codify this latest version of the game.

TAG RUGBY

Tag rugby is a cunning way of luring people into the game of rugby by removing the element of contact. Players are kitted out with a belt, to which two brightly coloured tags are attached with Velcro™. Players are tackled by removing one or other of the tags and waving it frantically in the air. The tackled player then has to stop and pass the ball to a teammate. Teams are allowed four consecutive tackles before they have to either score or pass possession to the other side.

In England, under a set of RFU regulations called the Rugby Continuum, tag is played exclusively up to the 'Under-8s' age group. Tackling is only introduced to children playing in the 'Under-9s'. At this point, some of the faster runners, who have dominated every game up till now, go off and join a football club.

Tag rugby also works well as a mixed adult game. If you don't have tag belts then touch rugby is much the same. Players are tackled by touching your opponent with two hands on their hips, below the belt.

RUGBY NETBALL

The Rugby Netball League was established in 1907 and is played on Clapham Common in South London during the summer. As the name suggests, scoring involves dropping the ball into a net at either end of the pitch. Players can pass in any direction and there are no offside laws. The pace is high and with a hard dry pitch, the tackles are extremely hard.

In spite of its name, unfortunately suggestive of a girls' high school game, it is no pastime for shirkers.

Archive press cutting (source unknown)

It's Not Just About the Players

The lads say my bum is the equivalent of one 'Erica'.

Bill Beaumont

INSTRUCTIONS FOR USE OF
A POLICEMAN'S HELMET

The combination of alcohol and rugby quite often seems to lead to random acts of public nudity. Australian Michael O'Brien was the first to remove his clothes at a major sporting event and, not surprisingly, it was a rugby crowd he chose to share his naked nether regions with as he took to the pitch during the England v France game at Twickenham in 1974. A policeman's helmet was famously used to protect his modesty.

Then, in January 1982, the 'Twickenham Streaker', otherwise known as Erica Roe, shot to fame during an England v Australia test match. Apparently the young and well-endowed Erica hadn't been planning to go to the game and was supposed to be at work in a bookshop in Petersfield, but was jollied into travelling by her older sister Sally. The two, amid a group of about twenty-five rugby fans, arrived at Twickenham and headed straight for the beer tent.

To avoid the attentions of a lecherous companion, Erica and a friend moved to the front of the stand, but by half-time were getting a little restless. Speaking to *The Observer* in 2001, Erica said, 'We were getting a bit bored, thought we should do something and within seconds had decided, "Let's streak".'

After passing her bra and packet of Marlboro cigarettes to some people behind her, she set off onto the pitch, to huge cheers from the crowd. Eventually a policeman caught up with her and did his best to protect her modesty. Unfortunately, on this occasion one policeman's helmet wasn't quite sufficient.

After a few public appearances and modelling offers from *Playboy* and *The Sun*, she gradually retreated to relative obscurity. She is now living happily in Portugal with her husband and three kids, and running an organic sweet potato farm.

The use of video evidence is not always conclusive, but it sure beats the memory bank of most witnesses.

Jack Gibson

SUPPORTER'S EQUIPMENT

- Hip flask

- Waxed jacket

- Club tie

- Beer vouchers

- Minicab phone number

Seated in the upper tiers of the stand at a rugby match, a spectator spots an empty seat much lower down, near the pitch on the halfway line. Taking a chance, he makes his way down and asks the man next to the empty seat it if there is anyone sitting there.

'It's all yours,' says the seated man, 'I was supposed to come with my wife, but she passed away. This is the first match we haven't been to together since we got married forty-five years ago.'

'I'm sorry to hear that. Couldn't you find a friend, relative or neighbour to use the seat?'

The seated man shakes his head. 'No. They're all at the funeral.'

GREAT STADIUMS

ELLIS PARK STADIUM, JOHANNESBURG

Home to the Springboks since 1928 and host to the 1995 World Cup final, Ellis Park is where the new, post-apartheid South Africa, with President Mandela watching in the stands, beat New Zealand in the final 15–12. It hosted seven matches in the 2010 football World Cup and has a capacity of 62,567.

MURRAYFIELD STADIUM, EDINBURGH

Murrayfield is the largest sports arena of any sort in Scotland and has been home to the Scottish national side and the Edinburgh club side since March 1925. In the days before all-seater stadiums, Murrayfield hosted the biggest crowd at a rugby match when 104,000 fans watched Scotland play Wales. With the seats in place, the capacity is now 67,130.

MILLENNIUM STADIUM, CARDIFF

Opened, as the name suggests, in time for the millennium celebrations, this ground is shared with the Welsh national football team and is the second largest stadium in the world. With a fully retractable roof and seating 74,500, it opened with a friendly fixture between Wales and South Africa, with Wales beating the Springboks for the first time ever.

Stade de France, Paris

Stade de France was built for the 1998 football World Cup and is shared by the national side and Stade Français, the Paris side that plays in bright pink shirts. It is the only stadium in the world to have hosted a rugby World Cup final and a football World Cup final and has a capacity of 81,338.

Twickenham Stadium, London

Back in 1907, a former market garden was purchased for £5,572 12s 6d. It is still occasionally referred to as Billy's Cabbage Patch after Billy Williams, the RFU committee member who made the original investment. The stadium was opened in 1909 and has been English rugby's headquarters ever since. The South Stand was demolished in 2005 and rebuilt, increasing its capacity to 82,000.

ENGLISH PREMIERSHIP CLUBS AND THEIR STADIUMS

Bath	Recreation Ground
Exeter Chiefs	Sandy Park
Gloucester	Kingsholm Stadium
Harlequins	Twickenham Stoop
Leeds	Headingley Stadium
Leicester Tigers	Welford Road
London Irish	Madejski Stadium
London Wasps	Adams Park
Newcastle Falcons	Kingston Park
Northampton Saints	Franklin's Gardens
Sale Sharks	Edgeley Park
Saracens	Vicarage Road

COMMENTATORS

Rugby commentators have to have the knack of explaining both the mechanics and the spirit and poetry of the game. Few have done it as well as the late Bill McLaren.

A few of his choice remarks:

On Phil Bennett: **'They say down at Stradey that if ever you catch him you get to make a wish.'**

On Jonah Lomu: **'I'm no hod carrier but I would be laying bricks if he was running at me.'**

'And it's a try by Hika the hooker from Ngongotaha.' (Wales v New Zealand 1980)

Meanwhile, down under there was a New Zealand rugby commentator who shall remain nameless, who once declared that, **'Andrew Mehrtens loves it when Daryl Gibson comes inside of him.'**

New Zealand commentator Murray Mexted, referring to a newly introduced law stating that once a player had been tackled to the ground he must let go of the ball immediately, said: **'I don't like this new law, because your first instinct when you see a man on the ground is to go down on him.'**

Other gems from Murray Mexted include:

'You don't like to see hookers going down on players like that.'

'He's looking for some meaningful penetration into the backline.'

And, when celebrating and promoting the skills and qualities of a player called Martin Leslie, he is reported to have said: **'Everybody knows that I have been pumping Martin Leslie for a couple of seasons now.'**

RUGBY IN FILMS

TOM BROWN'S SCHOOLDAYS (VERSIONS IN 1916, 1940, 1951, 1971 AND 2005)

Thomas Hughes' semi-autobiographical novel has been adapted no less than five times for the screen. Set, and often filmed, in Rugby School, it tells a tale of cruelty and bullying and features massive rugby games that look more like riots than sport.

THIS SPORTING LIFE (1963)

Starring Richard Harris, this gritty Northern drama tells the story of coal miner Frank Machin, who gets into a fight at a nightclub and ends up as the star of Wakefield Rugby League side. Featuring brutal violence on the pitch, and grim and miserable relationships off it, it's still a classic of its type and well worth watching.

IF... (1968)

A tale of revolution in an old establishment English public school. There are shots of a rugby match and an otherwise very proper lady baying for blood from the touchline. Features the famous line: 'There's no such thing as a wrong war. Violence and revolution are the only pure acts.'

Monty Python's The Meaning of Life (1983)

This includes a rugby match between the masters and the boys, in which the boys are subjected to ridiculous levels of violence from their sadistic teachers, and which then merges into scenes set in World War One.

Alive (1993)

Ethan Hawke stars in this true story, based on Piers Paul Read's 1974 bestseller, about the members of a Uruguayan rugby team forced to eat their dead companions to survive after their plane crashes in the Andes.

Up 'n' Under (1998)

An adaptation of the extremely funny play written by John Godber and the Hull Truck Theatre Company about an attempt to transform a group of deadbeats into a side that can beat the local champions from the Cobblers Arms.

Invictus (2009)

Tells the story of how the Springboks won the 1995 Rugby World Cup and emerged as an unlikely unifying force in post-apartheid South Africa. It stars Morgan Freeman as Nelson Mandela and Matt Damon as François Pienaar, and was directed by Clint Eastwood. Although some have criticised the realism of the rugby-playing scenes, the film captures the mood of the monumental transformation of South Africa into what Desmond Tutu described as a 'Rainbow Nation'.

EQUIPMENT

Rugby is a game for the mentally
deficient... That is why it was
invented by the British. Who else
but an Englishman could invent an
oval ball?

Peter Pook

ODD-SHAPED BALLS

From the sport's beginnings in the 1840s up to the late 1860s, rugby balls had a stitched leather exterior enclosing an inflated pig's bladder. The introduction of rubber bladders in 1862 by Richard Lindon enabled balls to be made in a more oval shape, making them easier to handle, and in 1892 the Rugby Football Union made the oval ball compulsory.

In today's game, perhaps more than ever, precision ball-play can mean the difference between defeat and victory; recognising this, many manufacturers look to make their balls more windproof, waterproof and foolproof. For the 2003 Rugby World Cup, regular match-ball suppliers Gilbert spent eighteen months developing a ball that was designed to be 'un-droppable'. Ironically, England went on to win the cup that year largely thanks not to the hands but to the feet (or, more precisely, the kicks) of one Jonny Wilkinson.

IRB OFFICIAL BALL STANDARDS

- Shape: oval, made of four panels

- Material: leather or a synthetic material; the material may be treated to make the ball water-resistant and easier to hold

- Length: 280–300 mm

- Circumference (end to end): 740–770 mm

- Circumference (width): 580–620 mm

- Weight: 410–460 g

- Air pressure: 0.67–0.70 kg/cm^2

PUTTING THE BOOT IN

Boots are the first investment any aspiring rugby player will need to make. Traditionally, forwards have opted for heavier boots with strong toecaps and high ankle support to protect their delicate feet from opposing studs. Backs will be found wearing brightly coloured cutaway boots with moulded blades instead of studs, and shiny, go-faster stripes instead of encrusted mud and dried blood.

STUDS

At the beginning of every game the referee will line up both teams and inspect their studs. This harks back to the era when rugby began, when it was played by men wearing their working or walking boots. The boots were often hobnailed and men were indeed known to add bits of metal to the sole. The practice of 'hacking over' i.e. trampling on your opponents' bodies, was a common feature of the game.

In 1889 the laws included the statement that 'No one wearing projecting nails, iron plates, or gutta percha [a durable latex plant derivative used in pistol grips and rifle shoulder pads] on any part of his boots shall be allowed to play in a match.' In their pre-match rituals nowadays, referees are just looking to check that there are no sharp edges on the boots.

Studs occasionally fall out and can be replaced and tightened using a stud key, which can usually be borrowed from an older player in the changing room.

GUMSHIELDS

Every player of organised mini or junior rugby will be forced to play with a lump of moulded plastic around their delicate upper teeth. This is to prevent injury to the face and jaw during contact.

Dentists can provide an individually tailored gumshield, which can be pricey but is comfortable for the wearer and reassuring for nervous parents. A cheap and cheerful option is the brightly coloured 'boil in the bag' version: these cost just a few pounds and are softened up in a mug of boiling water. You then mould them around your own teeth.

Of course the incompetent and disorganised will do both: buy an expensive bespoke shield, lose it somewhere between the kitbag and the washing machine, only notice two minutes before kick-off and then burn their gums on a hastily bought replacement.

There is far too much talk about good ball and bad ball. In my opinion, good ball is when you have possession and bad ball is when the opposition have it.

Dick Jeeps (1976)

SHORTS

Shorts are, of course, a fairly standard piece of kit, but second-row players have been known to wear shorts with strange handle attachments, enabling them to be hoisted in the line-out without entirely removing their reproductive abilities.

Jockstraps are rarely seen in changing rooms these days, with most players wearing cycling shorts or swimming trunks under their shorts. For the more serious and professional player, high-tech 'base layers' have been developed to keep that other sort of rugby tackle nestled in comfort and safety.

SOCKS

The more traditional club dress code may refer to stockings rather than socks. This is not an invitation to turn up for a game in fishnets. Save that for the annual club dinner.

SHIRTS

Traditionally shirts have been made of thick heavy cotton, seemingly designed to absorb as much mud, water and blood as possible. Lighter materials are more commonly used nowadays, in a tighter fit to give opposing tacklers less to grip onto and as an opportunity to showcase the rippling six-pack beneath.

The rugby shirt has made the transition from sportswear to fashion icon. It formed an essential part of the Sloane Ranger's wardrobe in the 1980s. Elegant and expensive versions have been produced by fashion designers like Clements Ribeiro and Ralph Lauren, and cheaper versions are manufactured in large numbers by high-street retailers. For some reason the fashion versions seem to sell in the smaller, slim-fit sizes. Real rugby players need a little more room inside.

HEADGUARD

Lightweight foam and Lycra™ protection for your skull. Often used by second-row players as a way of keeping their ears in place during the scrum, when they have their head wedged in between the backsides of the front row.

The downside is that it gives opposing players something else to grab onto and can get a little warm. The upside is that it can give you a little more confidence as you crash into a ruck or maul and reduces the chances of being sent off to casualty with concussion.

BODY ARMOUR

Snug Lycra™ underlayers with tactically placed layers of foam padding. Go easy on the shoulder pads if you don't want to look like something out of the 1980s American soap opera *Dynasty*. Otherwise can offer a discreet confidence booster and minimize the post-match bruises.

Rumour has it that the glossy adverts in magazines featuring professional players in their Lycra™ bodywear has much the same effect on women of a certain age as the *Grattan* catalogue lingerie section used to have on adolescent boys.

SHIN PADS

Essential protection for hookers, as their main job is to retrieve the ball when it is placed into the centre of the scrum and their opponents' main job is to stop them, or failing that, kick them in the shins.

DEEP HEAT™

The fragrance of choice for all players. A pungent ointment or spray used to relieve aches and strains. Works by giving nerve endings something else to think about other than the pain caused by previous matches or training injuries. You might also try Ralgex™ or Tiger balm™ for similar effects.

However, in spite of what older props might tell you, Deep Heat™ is not a medically approved alternative to a proper warm-up and set of dynamic muscle stretches.

THE SIX NATIONS

They were lucky to get nought.

Geoff Cooke after England's 11–0 victory
over France in 1989

ONE COMPETITION: SEVERAL PRIZES

THE CHAMPIONSHIP TROPHY – awarded to the team which scores the most points, with two points awarded for a win and one for a draw. A sterling silver trophy, first presented in 1993.

THE TRIPLE CROWN – only England, Ireland, Scotland and Wales are eligible for this one, awarded to any team that beats all the other home nations. Was referred to as the 'Invisible Cup' as there was no actual trophy awarded until sponsors RBS commissioned a silver platter in 2006.

THE CALCUTTA CUP – a separate trophy engraved with cobras and elephants by Indian craftsmen is awarded just to the winner of the England v Scotland game, the oldest international fixture in the world. The trophy was made from melted down silver rupees withdrawn from the bank account of the Calcutta Rugby Club as it disbanded due to the unplayable heat in the subcontinent.

LE CRUNCH – franglais title given to the annual clash between England and France by media and marketing types – inspired by the tough battles between the two packs.

CENTENARY QUAICH (pronounced 'quake' – but with a softer Scottish ending to the word, like at the end of 'loch') – Scotland v Ireland.

GIUSEPPE GARIBALDI TROPHY – Italy v France.

MILLENNIUM TROPHY – England v Ireland.

THE GRAND SLAM – no trophy at all but this is the big one, only awarded to a side that wins all five of its games.

THE WOODEN SPOON – awarded to the side finishing bottom of the table. No physical spoon is actually awarded. It is more of a concept, reflecting the shame and humiliation of coming last and borrowed from an old Cambridge University ritual of awarding one to the student who scraped a third-class degree by the smallest margin.

WOODEN SPOON

The heroic failure still celebrated in rugby (see above) led to the founding in 1983 of a children's charity called 'Wooden Spoon'.

As England had picked up the title after a dismal Six Nations campaign, a small group of travelling England supporters was ceremoniously awarded a real wooden spoon by a group of Irish fans. A charity golf match followed to see who would have the honour of keeping the spoon. The money raised paid for a school minibus and the charity was born.

The charity now has a few staff in an office in Surrey, forty regional committees and 11,000 members, and has handed out over £12 million to good causes.

AND THEN THERE WERE SIX

The Six Nations started life as the Home Nations Championship in 1883, involving just England, Scotland, Wales and Ireland. It was won for the first three years by England. France joined in 1910, making it the Five Nations Championship. Les Bleus failed to win a championship and dropped out in 1932. They rejoined in 1947 and jointly won the title with Wales eight years later in 1955. Italy are the latest arrivals, having joined in the millennium year. They had their best tournament so far in 2011, beating France 22–21 in Rome and narrowly missing out on beating Ireland.

SIX NATIONS WINNERS

2000	England
2001	England
2002	France (Grand Slam)
2003	England (Grand Slam)
2004	France (Grand Slam)
2005	Wales (Grand Slam)
2006	France
2007	France
2008	Wales (Grand Slam)
2009	Ireland (Grand Slam)
2010	France (Grand Slam)
2011	England

Note: Scotland won the last Five Nations Championship in 1999 before the arrival of Italy the following year.

Swing low, sweet chariot,
Comin' for to carry me home;
Swing low, sweet chariot,
Comin' for to carry me home.

I looked over Jordan,
And what did I see,
Comin' for to carry me home,
A band of angels comin' after me,
Comin' for to carry me home.

(Repeat chorus)

If you get there before I do,
Comin' for to carry me home,
Tell all my friends I'm comin' too,
Comin' for to carry me home.

African-American spiritual written by Wallis Willis sometime before 1862, and introduced to the Twickenham crowd by a group of boys from the Benedictine Douai School in Woolhampton. The public schoolboys led the singing after each try as England beat Ireland 35–3 in the last game of the 1988 season. The tradition has stuck ever since.

I knew he would never play for Wales ... he's tone deaf.

Vernon Davies, on his son's decision to play for England (1981)

They have this impression of English rugby that we all play in Wellington boots and we play in grass that is two foot long.

Clive Woodward

CLUBHOUSE ANTICS

A major rugby tour by the British
Isles to New Zealand is a cross
between a medieval crusade and a
prep school outing.

John Hopkins

SING UP, BOYS

Rugby clubs have had something of a reputation for raucous communal singing. With alcohol lubricating the voice box and loosening the inhibitions, rugby songs have emerged into a musical genre all of their own.

However, in recent decades the tradition has perhaps declined a little. Some blame drink-driving laws for emptying clubhouses before anyone has had a chance to drink enough to enable them to channel their own interior operatic tenor. Alternatively, it could have more to do with the fact that people actually get a lot drunker a lot quicker nowadays and are nowhere near coherent enough to remember more than one line of any song.

However, with the advent of ubiquitous smartphones making it possible for even the drunkest prop to download lyrics and tunes from the comfort of the bar, there may be hope that the tradition can be gradually restored.

IF I WERE THE MARRYING KIND

If I were the marrying kind,
Which thank the lord I'm not sir,
The kind of man that I would wed,
Would be a rugby full back.

And he'd find touch,
And I'd find touch,
We'd both find touch together.
We'd be alright in the middle of the night,
Finding touch together.

If I were the marrying kind,
Which thank the lord I'm not sir,
The kind of man that I would wed,
Would be a wing three-quarter.

And he'd go hard,
And I'd go hard,
We'd both go hard together.
We'd be alright in the middle of the night,
Going hard together.

Centre three-quarter... *pass it out*
Fly half... *whip it out*
Scrum half... *put it in*
Hooker... *strike hard*
Prop forward... *bind tight*
Referee... *blow hard*

DRINKING GAMES

BOAT RACE

Two teams line up on opposite sides of a long table, with their drinks in front of them. On the command 'go', the person at the head of each team downs their drink as quickly as possible and then places the empty glass upside down on their head. The next player then downs his drink and so on until each player has finished. The first team to all finish their drinks is the winner.

'TWENTY-ONES'

Counting game with obscure rules, that get harder to follow the drunker you get. Players sat around a table call out a series of numbers in turn starting with the number 'one'. Players then call out one, two or three consecutive numbers. If a player calls out a single number (i.e. 'two'), play continues in the same direction. If a player calls out two consecutive numbers (i.e. 'two, three'), the direction of play is reversed. If a player calls out three numbers (i.e. 'two, three, four'), the next player is missed out.

Play continues until someone makes a mistake, which is pretty common even when you are sober, or calls out 'twenty-one'. Players making a mistake, like playing out of turn, have to knock back two fingers worth of their drink. A player forced to say 'twenty-one' has to down the remainder of their drink. Players gradually add new random rules and the game usually descends into a bewildering chaos of shouting, cheering and drinking.

SPOOF

Each player has three coins. The players stand around in a circle and each one chooses to conceal one, two, three or none of the coins in the fist they are holding out. Players then have to guess the total number of coins that are being concealed by all the players in all the fists that are being held out. No two guesses can be the same. If someone guesses correctly, they are then out of the game. Other rounds follow and gradually more players drop out. The last person left in at the end is the loser and has to drink a forfeit.

We went wild, wild, wild – some of the guys went wilder than that.

Peter de Villiers on South Africa's victory over the All Blacks

ANDY POWELL AND THE GOLF BUGGY

Welsh international back-row forward Andy Powell may not have been the greatest ever player to pull on a red shirt for his country, but he has certainly played an important role in some of the post-match celebrations.

In the small hours of 13 February 2010, he was celebrating hard with his teammates after a dramatic victory against Scotland in the Six Nations tournament, when they had scored seventeen points in the final five minutes to win. For some reason, in what can only be 'forward's logic', he decided that a golf buggy would be the perfect vehicle for a quick trip to a service station for 'munchies'. Powell drove a mile and a half along the M4 before being stopped by police and breathalysed.

In court, Powell's lawyer said, 'Beer is a staple of any rugby side and here there was more than a few pints of beer... As soon as the police arrived, he realised he had made a mistake and without hesitation he accepted blame.' According to the prosecuting lawyer, what he actually said to the police was 'I'm an idiot, I know. Going down the M4 in a golf buggy, I'm a professional rugby player. What have I done?'

Naturally, and quite rightly, Powell was banned from driving and dropped from the international side, but he gave a few traffic policemen and sports reporters a laugh or two as they attempted to piece together the events following the night's celebrations.

A diminutive, young scrum half is in a nightclub on the Saturday evening after a tough game. An inebriated but well-endowed and enthusiastic young lady approaches him and invites him to dance.

'You'll have to excuse me. I'm a little stiff from rugby,' says the scrum half.

'It doesn't matter where you're from, darling,' replies the girl. 'It's what's in your heart that matters!'

WHAT GOES ON TOUR...

Most rugby clubs will have fond memories of adventures and encounters from the traditional end-of-season tour. Unfortunately few stories ever see the light of day because of the solemn law that declares, 'What goes on tour, stays on tour.' Whether it is the British and Irish Lions travelling to the southern hemisphere or a local amateur club's fourth XV having an end-of-season day trip to a side in a neighbouring county, the law of rugby *omertà* still applies.

Dorchester Gladiators, however, found that their exploits on their Easter tour to Romania in 2000 gained a wider audience than they had planned or expected.

Whilst some professional sides have added a macho-sounding name (Saracens, Barbarians, Sharks, etc.) to their geographical label for marketing purposes, when amateur sides do it, it normally signifies a bunch of rugby enthusiasts playing the game largely as a way of breaking up longer bouts of drinking. So it was when the Dorchester Gladiators set off to distribute toys to an orphanage in the former communist state.

A well-meaning embassy official took it upon himself to arrange a rugby fixture, but a misunderstanding somewhere along the line led to the national stadium being booked and a side packed with international players lining up against the British amateurs. Not only that, but the game was all set to be broadcast live on national television and played in front of a huge crowd.

Whilst the Romanians were warming up on the pitch, the terrified Dorchester side were nursing hangovers and nervously smoking cigarettes. Only once the game started did the Romanians realise the mismatch and, after scoring a succession of points, eased off the hapless visitors. The final score was 60–17 to the hosts.

RUGBY V FOOTBALL

Rugby – posh man's sport, of course. Fifteen men on a team because posh people can afford to have more friends.

Al Murray, English comedian

Rugby and football were essentially the same game until 1863 when the Football Association (The FA) was formed. Different clubs were playing to different sets of rules and a committee was convened to draw up a common way of playing. However, once they outlawed 'hacking', i.e. kicking your opponent in the shins, Blackheath Club refused to join and continued playing under Rugby School rules. The FA later went on to remove carrying the ball, and the two games went their separate ways.

Strangely enough, the only game where kicking your opponent in the shins continues to be a problem is in the Association game.

I prefer rugby to soccer.
I enjoy the violence in rugby,
except when they start biting
each other's ears off.

Elizabeth Taylor

RUGBY IS BETTER THAN FOOTBALL BECAUSE...

This is a perennial debate – which is the better game, rugby or football? Of course, we know the answer, but here are a few arguments you can use when dealing with fans of the so-called beautiful game:

- Footballers are feeble: a footballer in his opponents' penalty area is liable to fall over, writhing in agony, from the slightest movement of air caused by a nearby defender. A rugby player may take up to three or four people to stop him from getting over the try-line.

- Footballers are feeble II: it will take at least two concurrent injuries to force a rugby player from the pitch. Footballers will go off for anything from a grazed knee to a hair gel malfunction.

- Rugby fans can be trusted to drink before, during and after a game without starting a riot.

- Respect for the match official. If a referee in football attempts to enforce one of the rules, players will surround him, swear and complain. In rugby, the referee is addressed as 'Sir'.

- The oval ball, with its unpredictable bounce, tests the skill and dexterity of the players more than the plain old round one, and creates moments of drama and tension.

- Rugby players play for each other – footballers play for themselves.

- A decent rate of point scoring. You don't see many rugby games that finish nil–nil.

- A better class of singing from the terraces – 'Swing Low, Sweet Chariot' v 'You're Sh*t and You Know You Are'.

- Average ticket prices for Premiership football in England are around £30, and are often far higher than this. Average prices for Premiership rugby are more like £20.

- Rugby can field a united British and Irish side for the Lions Tour. The football home nations can't get together a GB team for the Olympics even when they are the host nation.

- England have won a rugby World Cup this century.

- The German national rugby side is ranked thirty-sixth in the world.

The tactical difference between Association Football and Rugby with its varieties seems to be that in the former, the ball is the missile, in the latter, men are the missiles.

Alfred E. Crawley (1913)

IS THERE A DOCTOR ON THE PITCH?

It's definitely the hardest tackle I've taken in my life but I'm still breathing and that's a good sign.

Derick Hougaard, South African rugby player

INJURIES

Researchers who followed the World Cup-winning England side in 2003 reported 218 injuries per 1,000 hours of playing time. This perhaps suggests that an England international player should expect to get injured on average once every three or four games. A study in Scottish schools found 10.8 injuries per 1,000 playing hours.

Although injuries are more likely to occur during matches, between twelve and twenty per cent of injuries are sustained during training.

The incidence of injuries seems to have doubled since the advent of professional rugby. This is perhaps attributable to the increased intensity of the game, overtraining and the ball being in play for more of the game.

Injuries are most likely to occur during tackles, with the person being tackled typically coming off worse. Injuries are less likely to be caused by foul play, with just nine per cent of all injuries attributed to this cause.

Injury rates and types vary according to position played. Openside flankers, number eights and outside centres tend to receive the highest number of injuries. Forwards tend to have more back and neck injuries, whereas backs are more likely to damage shoulders.

Traditionally, injuries to the mouth, teeth, jaw and neck were considered common. Evidence suggests that the widespread use of mouthguards has considerably reduced these sorts of injuries.

Set plays such as scrums and line-outs are not thought to be a major contributor to the number of injuries. Studies suggest they only cause somewhere between one and thirteen per cent of injuries. However, debilitating injuries to the spine are generally related to scrums or rucks. A front-row player can have forces of 1.5 tons exerted on his flexed neck. Fortunately, constant vigilance from coaches, regulators and referees has kept these sorts of injury levels low.

Sure there have been injuries and deaths in rugby – but none of them serious.

John 'Doc' Mayhew, former doctor to the New Zealand national rugby union team

BLOODGATE

On 12 April 2009 the English Premiership side
Harlequins were playing Leinster at the Twickenham
Stoop in the quarter-finals of the Heineken Cup, the
tournament that pits the very best European club sides
against each other. With a place in the semi-finals at
stake, Harlequins were behind by just one point with ten
minutes to play. What happened next was to effectively
end the career of one of the all-time rugby greats and
introduce a new '-gate' to the list of media scandals.
Substitute winger Tom Williams came on, replacing
the injured fly half Chris Malone. Chris Malone
himself had been on as a replacement for Nick Evans.
This left Quins without a recognised kicker on the
pitch and desperate for some last-minute points,
perhaps from a penalty or a drop kick.
Someone somewhere then came up with the idea of
getting the specialist kicker Evans back on the field,
but the only way to do that would be for him to come
on as a temporary blood replacement. A blood capsule
was smuggled into the mouth of Tom Williams and he
came off with a wink for his teammates, captured by a
Sky TV cameraman.
Complaints and inquiries followed, revealing that a
doctor had later deliberately cut Williams' mouth

in order to make the fake injury a real one. Dean Richards, the legendary former England and Lions number eight and Harlequins Director of Rugby, was given a three-year ban from having anything to do with the sport. Tom Williams had an initial twelve-month ban reduced to four for co-operating with the authorities in the inquiry. Harlequins were fined just over a quarter of a million pounds.

Dean Richards said afterwards, 'I took full responsibility for it. It was a farcical situation, it really was. It didn't pan out particularly well on the day.'

In my time, I've had my knee out, broken my collarbone, had my nose smashed, a rib broken, lost a few teeth, and ricked my back; but as soon as I get a bit of bad luck I'm going to quit the game.

J. W. Robinson

If I lie in hospital and I hear they are putting someone's head back on that was ripped off by Schalk then I'd say: 'That's Schalk, he plays aggressive but he's not malicious.'

Peter de Villiers on Schalk Burger

CAULIFLOWER EAR

Otherwise known as hematoma auris, perichondrial hematoma, or traumatic auricular hematoma, cauliflower ear occurs when the outer ear is hit and a blood clot or other collection of fluid collects between the cartilage and the nutrient-supplying layers around it. The cartilage then dies, leading to the formation of fibrous tissue, and the outer ear becomes permanently swollen and deformed.

It can be treated with antibiotics and cosmetic surgery but many players choose not to bother, considering a deformed ear to be a badge of honour. Psychiatrists researching towards the end of the 1800s thought that cauliflower ear was linked to insanity. Anyone who has spent much time with front-row forwards might be forgiven for thinking that those early shrinks might just have been onto something.

WARM-UP DRILLS

Before a game of rugby, or even a moderately intensive training session, there will inevitably be a warm-up drill. This is designed to limber up the muscles and joints and generally enhance performance and prevent injury.

Players at different levels and in different positions adopt a different attitude to the warm-up. Younger players often don't see the point, blessed as they are with the invincibility of youth. Older forwards sometimes prefer to save their limited energy for the game itself. Somewhere in the middle are those who know that a gentle stretch before the game will probably prevent a muscle being pulled during it.

The trend nowadays is towards something called dynamic stretching. Exercises designed to stretch the major muscle groups are incorporated into a routine involving running around in small groups. Leaps, bounds and lunges are combined with sideways running, high knee steps, heel flicks and squats.

Upper bodies are warmed up with a series of shoulder turns, neck stretches and arm contortions. Teams will line up in groups of four or five and run up and down passing the ball down the line. Adventurous ones will arrange themselves in opposite corners of a square and run across each other to warm up their brains as well as their muscles.

Whether it all makes a difference is up for some debate. Many is a time when an amateur team has arrived an hour or two early for a game and warmed up thoroughly, only to be beaten by a side whose only pre-match preparation appears to have been a pint and a cigarette.

However, sports science research is on the side of the warmer-uppers.

A 'cluster randomised controlled trial' of young female footballers in Norway found that the risk of injuries was significantly reduced in the groups which followed a comprehensive warm-up programme prior to matches and training. So if it works for Norwegian schoolgirls, it's probably worth at least the backs getting involved.

Five years ago, many of the England team were sick at half-time – such is the intensity of playing the All Blacks.

Lawrence Dallaglio, former English rugby player

The bone was out of place and I could feel something wasn't right. Fortunately, a few moments later I went on to tackle Hull's Steve Norton and my jaw caught his knee. The impact caused my jaw to click back into place and I was able to carry on.

Roger Millward, former English rugby player

TALKING A
GOOD GAME

A game played by fewer than
fifteen a side, at least half of whom
should be totally unfit.

Michael Green, *The Art of Coarse Rugby*

We've lost seven of our last eight matches. Only team that we've beaten was Western Samoa. Good job we didn't play the whole of Samoa.

Gareth Davies, former Welsh rugby player

I think Brian Moore's gnashers are the kind you get from a DIY shop and hammer in yourself. He is the only player we have who looks like a French forward.

Paul Randall (1994)

If you can't take a punch, you should play table tennis.

Pierre Berbizier (1995)

No leadership, no ideas. Not even
enough imagination to thump
someone in the line-up when the
ref wasn't looking.

J. P. R. Williams on Wales losing 28–9 against
Australia (1984)

I think you enjoy the game more if
you don't know the rules. Anyway
you're on the same wavelength as
the referees.

Jonathan Davies, former Welsh rugby player

We actually got the winning try three minutes from the end but then they scored.

Phil Waugh

Mothers keep their photo on the mantelpiece to stop the kids going too near the fire.

Jim Noilly on the Munster pack

I'm just off for a quiet pint; followed by fifteen noisy ones.

Gareth Chilcott, former English rugby player, after his last game for Bath

Rugby may have many problems,
but the gravest is undoubtedly that
of the persistence of the summer.

Chris Laidlaw, New Zealand writer, radio talk shop
host and former rugby player

The advantage law is the best
law in rugby, because it lets you
ignore all the others for the good
of the game.

Derek Robinson

Whoso would be a man, must be a non-conformist, and preferably play in the pack.

Ralph Waldo Emerson

The women sit, getting colder and colder, on a seat getting harder and harder, watching oafs, getting muddier and muddier.

Virginia Graham

You can go to the end of time, the last World Cup in the history of mankind, and the All Blacks will be favourites for it.

Phil Kearns

A forward's usefulness to his side varies as to the square of his distance from the ball.

Clarrie Gibbons

Bill, there's a guy just run on the park with your backside on his chest.

Steve Smith, as Erica Roe streaked at
Twickenham (1982)

The relationship between the
Welsh and the English is based
on trust and understanding.
They don't trust us and we don't
understand them.

Dudley Wood (1986)

There's a broad green field in a broad green vale,
There's a bounding ball and a straining pack;
There's a clean cold wind blowing half a gale,
There's a strong defence and a swift attack.
There's a roar from the 'touch' like an angry sea,
As the struggle wavers from goal to goal;
But the fight is clean as a fight should be,
And they're friends when the ball has ceased to roll.
Clean and keen is the grand old rule,
And heart and courage must never fail.
They are making men where the grey stone school
Looks out on the broad green vale.
Can you hear the call? Can you hear the call?
Now, School! Now, School! Play up!
There's many a knock and many a fall
For those who follow a Rugger ball;
But hark! – can you hear it? Over all –
Now, School! Now, School! Play up!

Eric Wilkinson, from 'Rugby Football'
First published in 1917

RESOURCES

WEBSITES

www.irb.com – the website of the International Rugby Board with up-to-the-minute world rankings and the laws of the game in seven different languages.

www.rfu.com – the official site of the Rugby Football Union, the governing body of the game in England, with links to help you get more involved in the game.

www.rugbyfootballhistory.com – an exhaustive history of the game with a comprehensive timeline and delightful stories and anecdotes, lovingly curated by Nigel Trueman.

www.bbc.co.uk/sport1/hi/rugby_union/skills – a handy set of top tips and guides from the professionals for improving your game.

BOOKS

Benson, Richard *Rugby Wit: Quips and Quotes for the Rugby Obsessed* (2007 Summersdale Publishers Ltd)

Daniell, John *Confessions of a Rugby Mercenary* (2009 Ebury Press)

Douglas, Derek *The Book of World Rugby Quotations: Wit, Wisdom and Wisecracks from the Rugby Union Game* (1991 Mainstream Publishing Company (Edinburgh) Ltd)

Gauge, Steven *You Know You're a Rugby Fanatic When...* (2010 Summersdale Publishers Ltd)

Griffiths, John *Rugby's Strangest Matches: Extraordinary but true stories from over a century of rugby* (2000 Robson Books, an imprint of Anova Books Company Ltd)

Hale, Bruce and Collins, David *Rugby Tough* (2002 Human Kinetics Publishers, Inc.)

Johnson, Martin *Martin Johnson: The Autobiography* (2003 Headline Book Publishing)

Woodward, Clive *Winning!: The Story of England's Rise to Rugby World Cup Glory* (2004 Hodder and Stoughton, a division of Hodder Headline)

MAGAZINES AND NEWSPAPERS

Rugby World – The world's best-selling rugby magazine

Rugby Times – Britain's longest established dedicated Rugby Union weekly newspaper

MUSEUMS

The Webb Ellis Rugby Football Museum, Rugby, Warwickshire: Opened in 1980 in the building where James Gilbert made the first rugby balls in 1842. Exhibits featuring original balls and pumps from the early years.
Open Monday to Saturday.

World Rugby Museum, Twickenham Stadium:
Tells the history of the sport with interactive displays. Replica of the Rugby World Cup won by England in 2003 on permanent display. Tickets include a stadium tour.
Open every day of the week except Mondays and match days.

www.summersdale.com